LOGICAL ANALYSIS OF I.T. CHANGES

ISBN: 978-1-4717-2288-2

Copyright   ©   Andreas Sofroniou`   2012

All rights reserved.

Making unauthorised copies is prohibited. No parts of this publication
may be reproduced, transmitted, transcribed, stored in a retrieval
system, translated in any language, or computer language, in any
form, or by any means, without the prior written permission of
Andreas Sofroniou.

Copyright   ©   Andreas Sofroniou`   2012

LOGICAL ANALYSIS OF I.T. CHANGES

ISBN: 978-1-4717-2288-2

CONTENTS: PAGE:

LOGICAL ANALYSIS OF SYSTEMS CHANGES

Change Management and the changes to Configuration, Release, and Assets as a whole group of activities have traditionally been concerned with finding effective solutions to specific operational problems. The purpose of this book is to look at current problems and new, better methods, techniques, and tools for processing changes. In the past, it has been found that too many of the solutions are not implemented and, of those that are, too few survive the inclination of client functional areas to return to familiar ways of doing things. Therefore, Change Management personnel have gradually come to realize that their tasks should not only include solving specific problems but also designing problem-solving and implementation systems that predict and prevent future problems, identify and solve current ones, and implement and maintain these solutions under changing conditions.

As an Executive in multi-national organisations and Government Departments, the author has come to realise that most problems do not arise in isolation but are part of an interacting system. The book, in principle, is seeking for a process of simultaneous interrelated solutions to a set of interdependent problems. Further more, substantial effort has been devoted in recommending a rational methodology for one, or the least possible processes, for future change management. Businesses need to find better ways of doing things, is often not nearly as great as is the need to maximize use of what is already operational. This book, therefore, has been addressing itself more and more to determining how to produce the willingness to change procedures suitable to the way people are willing to work and with processes that they are familiar with.

The book, which follows various consultancy assignments, considers the additional, more detailed recommendations, including strategic changes, training, convincing resources, meetings with people, development of workshops and exchanges of new ideas. The reader, therefore, must consider such points that absorb resources, excessive costs and incur a heavy workload for existing staff.

In the areas in which technology advances fastest, new products and new materials are required in a constant flow, but there are many client areas in which the rate of change can be gentle. Although each process considered may be trivial, the total effect is many times as large as the margin between success and failure in an operational situation. These efforts to improve existing processes have been formalised under the various sections of this book.

The legacy processes and their procedures have had a dramatic impact on the management of changes. The speed and data-handling capabilities of experienced staff, enables the realistic changes and because of their know-how they get meaningful solutions to those changes through the use of long standing techniques. The changes occurring under such circumstances consist of calculating the performance of a system by evaluating a model of it for randomly selected values of variables contained within a unique process and its procedures. Most changes under such operations are concerned with "stochastic" variables; that is, variables whose values change randomly within some probability distribution over time.

There is still considerable difficulty, however, in drawing inferences from operational legacy processes to the real world of smooth Change Management. Additionally, the growing number of changes in the information-processing applications is currently on the increase. To this effect, the recommendations made in this book may be the optimum solution to the problems of adopting new processes. The procedures recommended as processes, will improve the cost-effectiveness of changes and their management. In the realm of the economy, they may be expected to lead to higher productivity, particularly in the service sectors and related processes, decision-making, problem solving, administration, and support of clerical functions.

Awareness that possession of information on any changes is tantamount to a competitive edge is stimulating the gathering of information at national levels. Similarly, concern is mounting over the safeguarding and husbanding of changes to the proprietary and strategic information within the confines of a client, as well as within outsourcing companies. Administration-oriented information systems and the management of changes in client sites have as their objective the husbanding and optimisation of corporate resources, namely; employees and their activities, inventories of materials and equipment, facilities, and finances.

A client's administrative information systems and the Management Information Systems (MIS) focus primarily on resource administration and provide top management with reports of aggregate data. Executive information systems may be viewed as an evolution of administrative information systems in the direction of strategic tracking, modelling, and decision-making. Typically, Change Management consists of a number of processes, each supporting a particular function and changes, which may occur any day of the year.

Change Management processes concentrate on resource allocation and task completion of organized activities. They usually incorporate such scheduling methods as the Critical Path Method (CPM) or Program Evaluation and Review Technique (PERT).

The processes, with which the book is concerned, are first of all man-made. Second, some of them are small and simple to manage, or they are large and complex, depending on the changes required. Their component parts sometimes interact so extensively that a change in one part is likely to affect many others. It is, therefore, of primary importance that all the Change Management processes interact with all the functionalities. Otherwise, Change Management as a tool is of no significance. Processes may also vary depending on the amount of human judgment that enters into their operation.

PROGRAMME MANAGEMENT

Programme Management may have many responsibilities, but the most important of all is the ability to identify and positively execute plans to manage the changes threatening the objectives.

Through a process of structured interviews and plans the Assessment Analysis is used to highlight the specific requests for changes, which may turn into risks. During the interviews Assessment Analysis is used to capture the key changes from the interviewees.

In turn, the Assessment Analysis provides a life-cycle process, which highlights the primary prioritisation of the changes. In large, complex, and critical programmes, it is essential that a true prioritised report is available so that the imminent changes can be managed first.

The process commences by identifying the most important changes, which may become threats to a project. These are given priority, support and management expertise. Once the prioritisation exercise is completed, the participating people are notified and subsequently interviewed to bring out and capture any possible changes they may have.

Within a programme, projects are prioritised to ensure that those most critical to the programme's success are given priority to scarce resources.

CHANGE MANAGEMENT METHODOLOGY

The Management of Change allows the capture of collective knowledge and expertise from those involved on the project, in a form that facilitates the communication of changes, their assessments, and the pro-active management of the changes requested.

In essence, this is the mechanism by which the functions of Information Technology programmes and projects are held together as a result of the principles operating within the methodology for the management of change:

• Systematic: The varied Changes, their Assessments and the consequential Risks relating to or consisting of a system. Methodical in procedures and plans, these are addressed to those involved and deliberating within the parameters of their systems development responsibilities.

- **Integration:** The results being dependable on the mutual or reciprocal action which encourages those involved in the programmes and projects to communicate with each other and to work closely with a view to solving the threatening changes before they impact on the development of the system.

- **Generic:** The individuals involved maintain an approach, which relates and characterises the whole group of those involved in assessing the changes and attacking any threatening ones before they become risks to the development of the system. The end result being the avoidance of apparent problems within the pre-defined users systems requirements.

- **Methodology:** Following the system architects and the change management practitioners enable this. Simply follow the approved body of systems development methods, rules and management procedures employed by their organisation. For practical or even ethical reasons, it must be noted that with such a philosophy, it is seldom possible to fulfil all requirements of very large organisational systems.

- **Applications:** As such, Change Management is administered by putting to use such techniques and in applying the Change Management principles in the development of various applications will involve numerous and varied activities. A concrete issue in developing new applications is the problem of communication among the people involved, the motivation constantly needed for generic work, the ability to interact systematically and in using Change Management.

CHANGES TO I.T. PROGRAMMES

In general, the Management of Change, deals with the substitution of one thing or set of conditions for another, thus making something different from its previous condition, be it an alteration in state or quality, variety, variation, mutation.

More specific, in the Information Technology environment anything that becomes different, be it the performance of a system, the planning of new enhancements, the development of new systems and their various phases, the complete configuration and its assets, releases, all this require a structure approach.

Change Management in Information Technology Programmes Management, therefore, includes and enables any:

- Alteration,

- Modification,

- Conversion,

- Variance,

- Transformation,

- Remodelling,

- Reconstruction,

- Re-organization,

- Substitution,

- Replacement.

Any kind or type of change which may occur and affect a systems configuration, releases and assets, be it hardware, software or whatever the term of IT may represent.

This process spans the whole life cycle from initial concept and definition of business needs through to the end of the useful life of an asset or end of a services contract. Both conventionally funded and more innovative types of funded projects are included. This definition is consistent with modern supply chain management practices. The process is not limited to the purchasing function in companies and departments and is inherently multi-functional especially in large, complex and/or novel procurements.

CHANGE MANAGEMENT LEADER

The Change Management Leader proposes and agrees the scope of the Change Management processes, function, the items that are to be controlled, and the information that is to be recorded.

Develops Change Management standards, Change Management plans and procedures. Evaluates Change Management tools and recommends those that best meet the organisation's budget, resource, timescale and technical requirements.

Creates and manages the Change Management plan. Performs audits to check that the physical IT inventory is consistent with the Change Management Database Initiates actions needed to secure funds to enhance the infrastructure and staffing levels in order to cope with growth and change

CHANGE MANAGEMENT CYCLE

The concept being a simple one as shown in the diagram below:

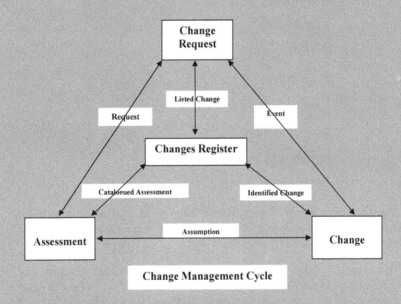

The Change Management principles explained in this book were developed by the author whilst employed by *PsySys Limited*, over a period of twenty four years. The methodology was used for PsySys'

international clients, from 1980 onwards. The idea of a structured approached to organisational requests for changes and their management proved beneficial to customers and users who integrated the full process with other methodologies, such as Structured Systems Analysis and Designing methods and Project Management procedures.

INTEGRATION OF METHODOLOGIES

The comprehension of how to integrate the three methodologies can be achieved, simply by following the concept as shown below:

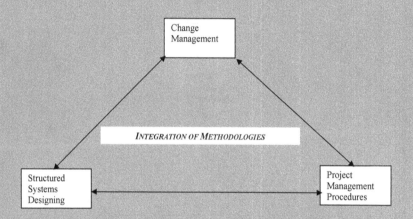

INTER-RELATIONSHIP

The various steps included in each of the methodologies are named in the next diagram. Or, to a further extent, the various stages of system development and the steps taken to manage projects and adopt the change management cycle, are shown on the next page:

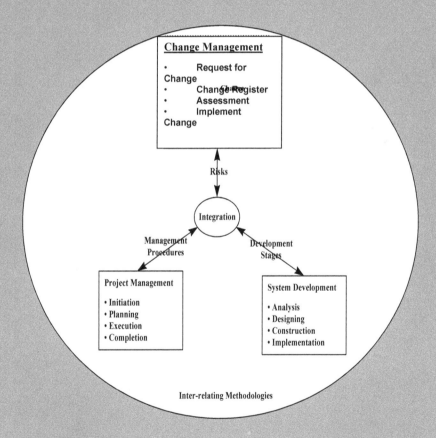

Change Management

* Request for Change
* Change Register
* Assessment
* Implement Change

Risks

Integration

Management Procedures

Development Stages

Project Management

• Initiation
• Planning
• Execution
• Completion

System Development

• Analysis
• Designing
• Construction
• Implementation

Inter-relating Methodologies

MANAGING THE CHANGE PROGRAMME

It is basic business sense to identify, assess, manage, and monitor changes that are significant to the fulfilment of an organisation's business objectives. In recent years businesses have been transformed by, and are in many cases heavily dependent on I.T.

The financial consequences of a breakdown in controls or a security breach are not only the loss incurred, but also the costs of recovering and preventing further failures. The impact is not only financial: it can affect adversely reputation and brand value as well as the business' performance and future potential.

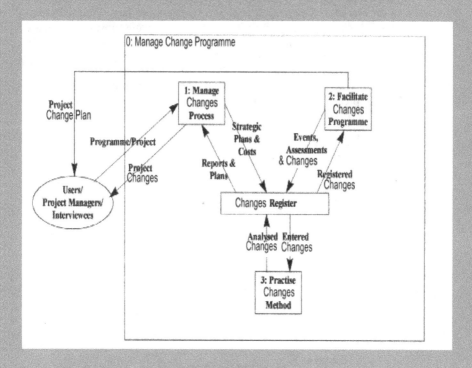

IMPACT ON BUSINESS

Boards can regard inadequate system development a— significant risk, and where directors feel that this may be the situation in their organisations, they may need to ask tough questions of themselves and their management teams. Systems development and their changes is an issue that boards may need to recognise should regularly be on their agenda, and not delegated to I.T. technicians.

Business in the past was primarily confined to assessment of the change and its associated risk surrounding fire, flood, and Acts of God. In business today we have become high dependent on information systems. Failure to build computer systems as required and the changes requested thereafter, by the users has a major impact on our business to function. The inability of companies to provide adequate systems can cause potential problems to customers, suppliers, employees and an all round havoc to information.

To build a complete picture of what the Change Management cycle includes, please refer to the diagram drawn below:

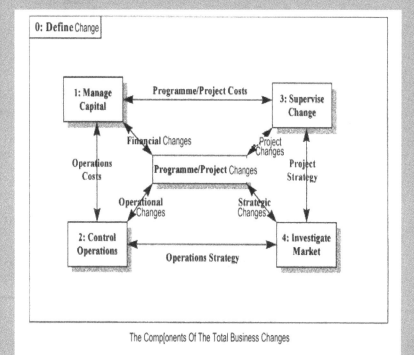

The Components Of The Total Business Changes

ASSESSMENT OF CHANGES

Fundamental to the creation of a Change Management system is the assessment of the changes (Changes Analysis) to your business and the potential loss that could accrue if things go wrong. Change Assessment software tools are available in the market, which can be used by consultants, or by internal staff. What is important is the ability to assess the change to your business and the cost to protect it against the change. The end result is that you have to make the valued judgement on the amount the business spends, on the implementation and the monitoring of a change policy.

Products and systems are available to counter the threats and changes that have been identified. There is a wide range of options available, but remember that anything chosen will require expertise to design and complete a system, taking into account how the various solutions will inter-react with each other. Like all things to do with I.T., the design and implementation of systems, change solutions are only as good as the people installing them.

COMMUNICATION

The most important factor in the success of any management style is the ability to communicate with each other, one to one or in groups of people. The art of communication is just as important to the whole process of the management of changes. More so, where the changes identified have become a threat because of the problem of human communications.

This is where the appointment of an experienced and trained Change Practitioner is worth the effort put into securing such individual/s.

CHANGE MANAGEMENT PRACTICE

A trained Change Management Practitioner will have enough knowledge to run and maintain the system, as well as ample experience to be able to communicate with all levels of employees, hold meetings, and ensure the plans executed.

In brief and as the diagram on the next page shows, the Practitioner will be responsible for the complete Change Management cycle.

CHANGE MANAGEMENT CYCLE

In analysing changes, certain counter measures may have to be looked into. The mechanisms for safeguarding the construction of your information system are by managing changes and avoiding the threat of failing to build the required system.

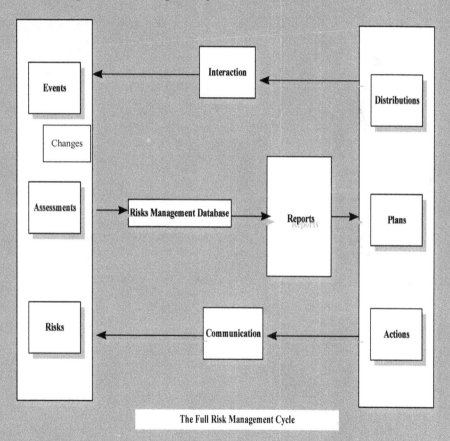

The Full Risk Management Cycle

PROGRAMME OBJECTIVES

It is a fact that most large, complex projects and programs fail to meet their planned objectives and as a consequence, most organisations are undertaking one or more aggressive programs at any point in time. These may fundamentally change the way the company conducts its business and failure to meet objectives on time may lead to a catastrophic loss of business.

Some projects or programmes can be chaotic at times. Objectives are evolving and plans and priorities are constantly changing. There is a temptation to accept this chaos as a necessary 'nature of the beast'. However, it is essential to move the programme forward in a traditional project management way by making sure that objectives and plans move forward.

Once we have clear objectives and plans, programme managers must control two fundamental factors if they are to be successful:

- The business plan must be clearly identified,

- The implementation of the program must be made explicit.

This can be answered by isolating the fundamental cause of most, if not all-major project problems. It can be argued that projects only fail due to two fundamental reasons:

- The plans are proven to be incorrect,

- The significance of these plans is misunderstood.

The capture, analysis, and communication of such assessments are, therefore, critical to the success of any project. This forms the basis of the Change Management method. This method has been applied by PsySys Limited to help many diverse organisations to deliver large, complex projects and programmes on time, to budget and in meeting the expectations of demanding users.

SUGGESTED METHOD

The focus of the method is based on he capture and analysis of the critical events and their assessments within the project plans, processes, and procedures.

The method is essentially a framework process that allows the capture of collective knowledge and viewpoints from those involved on the project, in a form that facilitates communication of events, assessments and ensures the pro-active management of changes. This is accomplished by dramatically improving communications, risks (which may be caused by changes) are avoided or managed to the optimum, and project objectives are delivered on time.

In essence, this is the mechanism by which the functions of programmes and projects are held together as a result of the principles operating within the method.

This, in effect, includes the varied events, their assessments and the consequential changes relating to or consisting of a system. Methodical in procedures and plans, these are addressed to those involved and deliberating within the parameters of their systems development responsibilities.

The results being dependable on the mutual or reciprocal action which encourages those involved in the programmes and projects to communicate with each other and to work closely with a view to solving the threatening events before they impact on the development of the system.

The individuals involved maintain an approach, which relates and characterises the whole group of those involved in assessing the events and attacking the threatening ones before any changes become risks to the development of the system.

Following the system architects and the change management practitioners enables this. Simply follow the approved body of systems development methods, rules and management procedures employed by their organisation. For practical or even ethical reasons, it must be noted that with such a philosophy, it is seldom possible to fulfil all requirements of very large organisational systems.

As such, the suggested method is administered in the various applications. Putting to use such techniques and in applying the change management principles in the development of various applications will involve numerous and varied activities. A concrete issue in developing new applications is the problem of communication among the people involved, the motivation constantly needed for generic work, the ability to interact systematically and in using a structured systems methodology.

CHANGE MANAGEMENT CYCLE

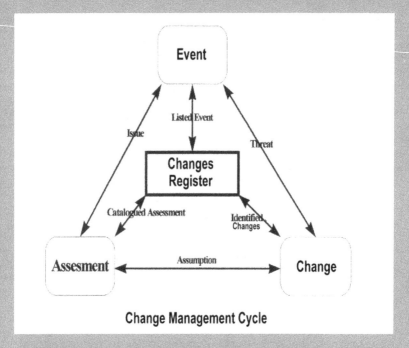

Change Management Cycle

FEATURES OF THE APPROACH

The key features and benefits of the PsySys Limited approach are:

- *Communication* — Provides a simple, common, language for the communication of risk up, down and sideways within the organisation, whilst avoiding the normal problems of political sensitivity and risk aversion.

- *Control* — Enhances project control by exception management and achieves an overview of change at senior management levels.

- *Information* — Encourages the sharing of change information, establishing common objectives, discouraging change transfer and hence reducing the overall risk to all involved parties.

- *Flexible* — An adaptable process, which is rigorously applied to ensure that all significant changes are identified and controlled at the appropriate time.

- *Acceptable* — The non-intrusive/non-bureaucratic management process improves management discipline across the organization and is readily accepted by project teams.

ASSESSMENT ANALYSIS

The core of *Change* is in the Assessment Analysis. This uses structured techniques to analyse project plans and identify the most sensitive events that are potentially unstable, and therefore the source of greatest change.

Everything is rated on a GAR principle: Green, Amber and Red scale; where G is always "good" and R is always "bad". This provides an instantly understood assessment on each stage: Events, Assessments, and Changes in relationship with the time scales as used in the plans. This, effectively, provides guidance on how best to handle the change.

STRATEGIC COST ANALYSIS

Costing is a process within the approach that can be used to define the cost of a requested change within a project or business area from as early as the proposal stage. It works by adding a 'quality' dimension to the estimating process so that high quality estimates, based on relevant experience, are treated differently from low quality estimates, which are little more than guesses.

The output takes the form of a probability distribution diagram and a set of assessments, which need to be managed in order to move the curve to the left and squeeze it (i.e. reduce the likely cost and the uncertainty).

Costing is particularly useful in the early stages of a project when the final cost of the project is subject to great uncertainty. The process has also been effectively used to define business budgets for re-structured business areas.

ADMINISTRATION SYSTEM TOOL

A Microsoft Access based tool or any type of an ordinary spreadsheet can be utilised to allow the events, assessments and changes to be captured and reviewed by all stockholders in the program. In this way changes that would have been missed are captured through the identification of events.

WORK PLAN ANALYSIS

Work Plan Analysis is a set of techniques that enables a rapid change assessment to be undertaken on a complex project, which is already in progress.

It is always difficult to focus on the right areas when the project organisation is large and the plans are extensive and likely to be multi-levelled. Using Work Plan Analysis, the 'poor quality' areas of a project are quickly highlighted for further investigation.

One very successful application of this approach has been through the use of Project Readiness Assessment Walkthroughs. These are structured review meetings held just prior to major project milestones or deliverables. Initially the project team explain their self-evaluation of the project status and are questioned by an independent review team. Potential changes arising are captured using the Assessment Analysis process.

COMMUNICATING CHANGES

The technique summarised above will only deliver its full benefits to any business if a suitable governance structure is quickly established to communicate the change information and set suitable actions to mitigate the changes. The mapping of the process onto an organisation is the key step to ensuring that the investment in the process is fully realised.

TEAM APPROACH

An enterprise must escape from a culture based on transfer of changes between parties, to a team approach that is focused on implementing changes. Methods must be effective without the need for detailed time-consuming analysis.

DEFINITION OF A CHANGE

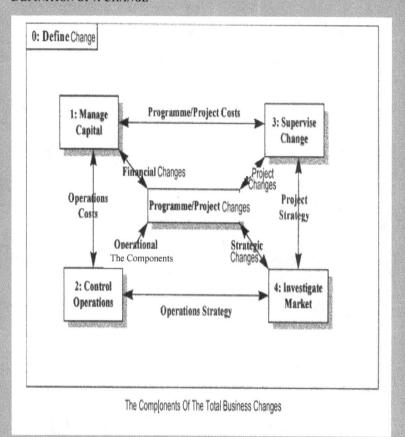

The Components Of The Total Business Changes

A change may be perceived as a possible loss. A change is individual to a person or organisation because another as a minor change may perceive what one individual as a major change perceives.

A change is linked very strongly with competitiveness. Each decision has the possibility of resulting in loss. Each decision to introduce a new product into the marketplace can result in varying degrees of loss or gain. To be entrepreneurial is to accept change, that is, the possibility of loss. A good entrepreneur's strength, however, is to make decisions which maximise possible gain. Hence minimise possible loss, which constitutes effective change management.

Change is inherent in all aspect of an organisation and may be viewed from four primary directions: financial, operational, programme/project and portfolio/products. Many changes are related to the running of the operations and its processes but are often in trying to change operations that the greatest change is experienced. It is the management of change in such 'change' projects that the method (explained earlier) addresses.

A project can be described in its simplest terms as: Planning to achieve specific objectives and then executing the plans. The emphasis is on the word 'plan' as without a plan we have no project. So in the context of a project, a change is something, which might disrupt the plans such that the objectives of the project are not met. The discipline of Project Change Management is thus a framework of techniques, which allows the project manager to pro-actively identify and manage changes before they develop into problems, which will impact the project plans.

APPROACHES TO CHANGE MANAGEMENT

In recent years we have seen large projects in many areas of business suffering from a lack of control. The size of cost and time over-runs do not seem to be decreasing, despite the amount of management time which is being dedicated to analysing and quantifying the potential problems and selecting suitable personnel and processes. One may conclude that management, either do not have the correct methods and tools in place to attack the potential problems, or that they are not using, or do not understand, those which they do have.

In the early 1970's, the concepts of formal project change management began to emerge. Hailed as the saviour of project managers, in practice the results have been mixed. Change management has proved highly effective in certain mature industries - e.g. the Petrochemical or construction industry where project managers can base their estimates on years of similar engineering experience. Difficulties seem to be encountered when these traditional Change Management methods are applied to innovative and fast evolving areas such as Information Technology.

EVENTS AND CHANGE REGISTER

Most projects will have an Events Register and some may have what they call a Change Register. In effect, this tends to be a list into which anyone can input the concerns. It will contain references to current problems, questions, and assessments, difficult activities about which there is reasonable confidence and the odd real change.

In any large project the Events or Change Register quickly becomes swamped with items that require very different actions and many which do not require any action at all. All this leads to an inevitable loss of focus. Further, the content tends to be biased towards current problems rather than future potential problems.

INDIVIDUAL INTERVIEWS

One-on-one interviews can be an effective way of capturing changes. When management and peers do not inhibit people, they tend to be far more open about their concerns. Unfortunately, most use very unsophisticated approaches such as "what do you see as your changes?" or "what keeps you awake at night?" Thus, if the person being interviewed is sensitive to discussing changes it may prevent the capture of any valuable information. At best the changes captured will tend to lack structure, as they are not focused onto the future objectives that the project plans to achieve.

GROUP BRAINSTORMING

Can be a very effective technique for opening up a very complex situation. However, information can be subconsciously suppressed by peer pressure, which may bias the discussion on one area at the expense of the rest of the project. Inevitably the mass of information captured is often difficult to focus, prioritise and allocate ownership.

In general, it should be remembered that the quality of the output is only as good as the quality of the input data.

CHANGE ANALYSES AND QUANTIFICATION

Changes may be difficult to capture reliably and concisely but further problems are likely to be experienced when trying to analyse them. Virtually all approaches to change analysis are based on estimating the factored impact of the change. This exposure to change is a combination of the chance (probability) of an event happening and the consequences (impact) if it does occur i.e.:

- Change Exposure = Potential Impact x Probability of Occurrence

Fundamental problems arise when individuals are required to estimate, numerically, the impact and then predict (numerically) the probability. Estimates, which are often little more than guesses, result in a single point estimate of Change Exposure, which is then given undeserved credibility in the detailed analysis of the change and used as the basis for many major project decisions. Also, it is often the case that part of the change impact can be quantified but often not the major part. An example can be based on an attempt to quantify bad publicity, quality, and relationship.

Some processes add complexity by rating the impact of changes in terms of financial, time scales, quality, performance etc., which quickly become very tedious to maintain.

CHANGE CONTROL AND LACK OF FOLLOW-THROUGH

Many change management systems fail due to a lack of follow-through on actions. There is a surprising tendency to identify changes and then watch them happen!

This is caused by:

• Failure to use the change register to set appropriate action plans,

• Lack of regular updates/maintenance of the change register,

• Absence of named owners and deadlines (lack of ownership),

• Tracking generalities rather than specifics,

• Concentrating on what can be done if the change occurs rather than stopping the change happening (pro-active),

• Trying to transfer the change elsewhere, without considering the consequences.

CHANGE TRANSFER

Change transfer often occurs because the partner who knows most about the level of change within the enterprise (i.e. the supplier/purchaser relationship) is encouraged to transfer this to the other partner. Once accomplished, the party with the most knowledge of the change relaxes and the most ignorant partner inherits the change. An example of this is the Purchaser insisting on a fixed-price contract in a poorly defined contract when they know that the supplier does not understand the scope of the contract.

The supplier then has a tendency to deliver the minimum possible and obtain sign-off for everything, irrespective of quality. The effect of this type of commercial 'table-tennis' is actually to increase the level of change within the enterprise as the real changes pile up without intervention.

What is needed is a method that identifies and encourages the attack of real change at source. Such a method would force projects within the enterprise to become pro-active by attacking risky changes, rather than waiting for events to unfold and then counting the cost, as recorded in the previous month's financial returns.

CHANGE MANAGEMENT VS. PROJECT MANAGEMENT

There is often a tendency to treat change management as no more than another necessary evil of project management. Thus, it often becomes an additional administrative burden for the Project Manager and consequently does not get the quality attention to make it work effectively.

In order to make change management work, a shift in philosophy is required. This must lead the project team to view the process not just as another component of project management, but more as the communication stabiliser that holds the project together.

PROCESS METHOD

The Change Management method described in this book aims to provide an effective means of managing changes within all types of projects. The process grew out of a thorough assessment of the problems often encountered in project management and the techniques of the traditional change management approaches that have been used to try and improve the situation.

Both good and bad principles were noted and new techniques were introduced to address key deficiencies. The resulting change management process has a proven track record of delivering tangible results in large projects across a diverse range of organisations.

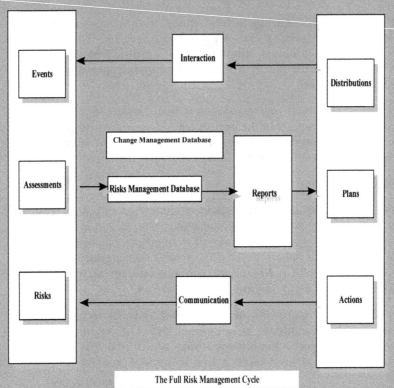

The Full Risk Management Cycle

Change

The full Change Management cycle.

EFFECT OF CURRENT PROJECT STATUS

The stage and status of the project will have a strong bearing on the change management initiation process. Although all situations are unique, the following may give some helpful guidelines. Such a status may make a Strategic Cost Analysis very attractive. If there are no plans it may be difficult to undertake a full Assessment Analysis, but a high level assessment of issues or assumptions based on major milestones should be possible. Expect to identify a high proportion of changes that relate to missing or inadequate plans and resources problems. Projects just starting tend to have many events and few assessments (due to the lack of documented plans).

PLANNED PROJECT

Once the project has been substantially planned and is active, Assessment Analysis becomes the primary change identification process. If the planning is very detailed and/or complex, some of the techniques of Work Plan Analysis may prove useful. For example, if there were a requirement to produce a first-cut of a change register very quickly, for a rapidly approaching milestone, a Project Readiness Walkthrough would be an ideal approach.

TROUBLED PROJECT

The key aspect of a project in trouble is that it requires re-planning to put it back on track. Thus, the timing of the change assessment relative to this planning process is very important.

If the re-planning process has not started there will be very little of the new approach to assess. It may be possible to influence this new approach by undertaking a change assessment of the options being considered. To do this an Assumption Analysis of the alternative high-level plans can provide a useful framework for decision-making.

If the project has been re-planned, then an Assessment Analysis of the new plans, possibly supplemented by Work Plan Analysis, is an appropriate way forward.

INTERVIEWING KEY PEOPLE

Identifying the right people to interview is critical to producing a comprehensive and coherent picture of the changes facing a project. So, to decide on who should be interviewed, start with the project or programme organisational structure.

Depending on the scope of the change assessment (i.e. single project, programme of multiple projects, portfolio of business projects etc.) it may be necessary to map the organisational hierarchy to ensure that the right people are interviewed and that the changes arising are reviewed at an appropriate level.

Working with the Programme or Project Manager, try to identify the 'key players'. A key player is someone within the programme/project who is likely to have either specific expertise in a particular area and/or insight into the environment in which the project is being implemented.

Key players tend to be Project Managers for a programme or Team Managers for a project with the addition of Users involved in the requirement capture and other activities. This group would likely form the initial interview list.

During the interview, these people should decide who else is needed to participate. Interviewers need to exercise their judgement when evaluating the responses to this question. Typically it is necessary to go down at least one level below the Project/Team manager unless the team size is small.

One of the key features of this process is that of obtaining counter viewpoints within the organisation. Thus, the more people interviewed the better. However, if many projects are being assessed for change within an organisation, resource constraints will inevitably lead to reducing the interview pool. Under these circumstances at least two counter viewpoints must be obtained within each project. (Business manager and technical manager) so that the assessment ratings can be compared.

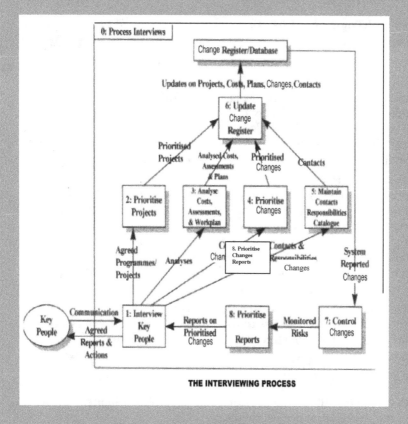

THE INTERVIEWING PROCESS

SUITABLE CHANGE ASSESSMENT TEAM

- The team that will operate and manage the process requires a particular set of skills and background to be successful:
- Experience of working in large (preferably non-consulting) projects and managing (preferably) medium sized projects (say 10-20 people).
- Understanding of project planning principles and some exposure to associated tools.
- Forceful personalities to ensure quality data captures in difficult client situations.
- IT background, in order to understand the issues in IT projects and to help with using the support tools.
- Some understanding of the clients business.

Note that it can sometimes be a disadvantage to have too much knowledge of the clients business in applying the process. This is because there may be a tendency for the interviewer to get into too much detail in non-risky areas and take too much of the client's time in the process.

CHANGE REVIEW MEETINGS

After the initial round of interviews, a suitable forum must be established to discuss the changes identified. The client may suggest that the changes are discussed as part of the regular project meeting. This should be resisted unless the changes are an early agenda item and there will be sufficient time to get through the agenda with this additional discussion.

Typically, a minimum of an hour will be required for discussion of the changes - all if possible but just the most critical if not. If discussion of the changes is left to the end there will often be little time (or concentration) left to do the process justice. Also, it is likely that some events will end up being discussed twice. If discussed first, the changes tend to focus the meeting and get away from talking about progress onto the things that need to be discussed - i.e. what threatens the success of the project.

The best method is to establish a specific Change Review Meeting with a representation consisting of the Change Owners and chaired by the Programme Director, or the process 'champion' in the client organisation.

CHANGE PRIORITISATION

Prioritisation allows the Project Manager to direct limited resources at the most critical project changes.

The objective of the change prioritisation is to identify the most significant changes out of all those, which have been identified by the various analysis methods used. Once all the changes have been collected in a consolidated list or register, they should be placed in order of priority and attacked via a logical, planned programme. The problem is to decide how to place changes in an appropriate order.

ASSESSMENTS AND CHANGES REGISTER

All assessments captured should be held in an Assessments Register. Only critical assessments will be converted into changes and held in a Change Register. Filtering the assessments and consolidating them into changes do this. All information captured will be rationalised and details of their source and consequences will be traceable.

POSITIONING CHANGES

The primary criteria used for prioritising changes are:

- Criticality
- Timing
- Controllability

CRITICALITY

In certain instances the change may undermine the basic objectives of the project and no amount of money will save the project if such a change impacts. If not resolved, the uncertainty may halt the progress of the project. Such a change may be related to the overall programme, a part of the programme, an individual part of the design, or even a particular module of software. This, also, provides a way of representing the effect of such changes on the overall project, where cost impact is small or meaningless.

To satisfy this need a Criticality index is defined. Criticality is in effect a multi-dimensional change impact rating. Once again, we use the assessment A, B, C. C being dangerous, while A impacts the edge of the system design or the programme. Something that may be important in itself, or to one group of users, or designers, but will not stop progress on the rest of the project.

In most applications, Criticality has been the primary means of prioritising changes and has been described in terms of traffic-light ratings of Red, Amber, or Green. This can be very effective at concentrating on the project impacts and/or avoiding confusion with ratings of assessment Sensitivity.

TIMING

One of the most important things we need to know is *when* we have to do something about an event, assessment, or change. In the case of a project we need to know when the change will start to impact the work. Then we must determine when we have to take action to prevent it happening or to reduce its impact. The timing of a change should always equate to the latest time to start the first necessary action. In this respect, it is analogous with trying to stop a cancer. This must be done at the point that it starts to grow.

CONTROLLABILITY

Controllability is a measure of confidence that the change will be managed. It should not be confused with the probability of the change occurring, which is a measure of how likely the change is to occur if nothing is done. The controllability grade cannot normally be assigned until the change has been reviewed and discussed by senior management, whereby an agreement is reached as to their confidence that the change can ultimately be managed. A 'C' grade means that no change plans are in place and no action has been taken, whereas an 'A' grade indicates that change plans or actions are well under way with a very high confidence of success.

CHANGE REGISTER REPORTS

Impact Diagrams provide an overview or change profile of the project. However, the detail of the changes is required for the change review meeting in order that the detail of the changes can be seen, discussed and actions taken.

The order of the changes in the report is important so that senior management can focus on the key changes first.

If the impact diagram is used to prioritise the change register the time element can be easily included. For instance there may be an urgent AMBER criticality, C controllability change that needs attention that is not an obvious priority if the Change Report is prioritised by Criticality and Controllability alone.

In essence the easiest way to prioritise is to use the Impact Diagram and to treat the highest priority change as the one nearest to the origin, the next nearest being number two and so on. The intention is to order the risks so that they are roughly in the right order.

CHANGE CONTROL

Changes may be attacked at both the strategic and tactical levels. Strategic approaches look for trends and underlying causes for groups of changes. Tactical approaches take each change at face value.

STRATEGIC APPROACHES

A strategic viewpoint is achieved by using the Change Driver approach. Each assessment and subsequent change is categorised into Technical, Milestone, Decision or Resource to reflect what is driving the poor quality ratings:

•   Technical relates to assessments of a technical or complexity nature (e.g. the pure complexity of providing an interface)

•   Milestone that applies to assessments regarding timescale dependencies on other projects, or external suppliers, and can be used to identify linkages to project milestones (e.g. an activity which is not inherently complex but may not be feasible due to timescale constraints).

- Decision that is used to describe assessments that require business decisions, business policies or standards (e.g. organisational announcements).

- Resources that relate to resource deficiencies or priorities (e.g. insufficient training resources).

Note that with this categorisation, Policy has been split into Decision and Resource categories. This is necessary when the resource constraints are external to the programme/organisation. When the resource constraints are internal, a simple Policy Driver will cover this.

Categorising assessments and changes in this way identifies the main change drivers, can simplify the identification of trends and assist in the development of appropriate change plans.

For example, Red Decision and Resource changes are "show-stoppers" which generally require senior management action. Red Milestone changes are an indication of how tightly the programme is being "squeezed" and Red Technical changes indicate the complexity of the planned activities.

The Change Driver chart indicates where particular effort is required. In the example below the relatively high number of Decision based changes suggests that the project is being put at risk by having to wait for decisions, probably from within the organisation. A steering committee meeting could potentially resolve most of these changes. If the project is in the early stages, it is already showing signs that the time scales are too ambitious by the high number of milestone changes.

	Technical	Milestone	Resource	Decision	Total
Red	7	15	4	19	45
Amber	12	19	15	26	72
Green	10	6	12	12	40
Total	29	40	31	57	157

It is important to note that noting that the "normal" Change Driver profile trends with the phase of the project. i.e. "Normal" would be (using relative terms):

Phase	Technical	Milestone	Resource	Decision
Start of project	Rising	Min.	Max.	Max.
Middle of project	Max.	Rising	Falling	Falling
End of project	Falling	Max.	Min.	Min.

TACTICAL APPROACHES

Most changes will need to be addressed specifically (i.e. one action plan for each change) to address the underlying assessment. Assessments that are placed in the C area of the Sensitivity/Stability matrix are unreliable, represent significant risks, and it is dangerous to continue with the project without taking action. We must do at least one of two things:

• Stabilise them by escalating the assessment to senior management and obtaining agreements that increase confidence that the assessment will turn out to be true.

• Make the project less sensitive to the assessment i.e. Reduce sensitivity by redesign, re-planning or having acceptable fallback plans in place.

The actions taken to attack the problem may be very different, depending on whether we are trying to reduce Sensitivity or Stabilise. It is normal to try to stabilise the assessment first before trying to handle sensitivity, which is usually more difficult.

FOLLOWING THROUGH ON ACTIONS

Just as it is possible to introduce change by planning a project badly, it is possible to address many changes by using normal project management methods, as long as the risk has been identified early enough.

Changes generally come from two areas activities that have not been planned adequately or planned activities that are likely to go wrong. Therefore, the first filter to apply to the changes is to identify those that can be tackled by just improving the plans. Obviously, if there is no project plan the change is unbounded and the first action must be to create a plan.

NEED FOR CHANGE PLANS

Changes, which cannot be resolved by improved planning, must be tackled individually through the use of dedicated Change Plans. Ultimately, the plans for reducing the changes must be incorporated into the main project plans.

Change Plans may be divided into "Simple" or "Complex", irrespective of the potential impact of the change. Simple means that it is possible to resolve the change quickly say by a simple phone call or single task. For such changes, monitoring the status on the Change Report is sufficient and minimises bureaucracy. Complex changes require significant resources and time to resolve them and for these a formal Change Plan is required.

DIAGRAMMATIC REPRESENTATION

The diagrammatic flow shown below is the desired overall integration of related top-level processes:

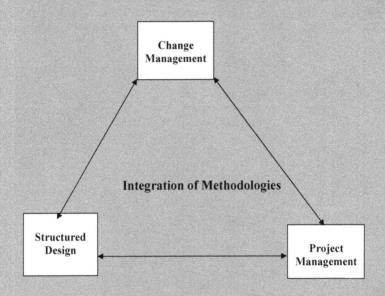

SUGGESTED INTERFACING

The suggested interfacing of the Structured Systems Analysis and Design methodology and the Project Management procedures to the Change Management processes may be done separately.

USING EXISTING METHODS

In interfacing the various processes from the different existing organisational methodologies, the main steps of Project Management and the Structures Systems Analysis and Designing methodology, will be incorporated in this exercise.

Namely, the four main stages of system development:

- **Analyse,**

- **Design,**

- Construct,

- Implement.

The identified processes of Project Management procedures and Structured Systems Analysis and Designing to be linked to the Change Management processes of:

- Events,

- Assessments,

- Changes,

- Plans.

The actual points of interfacing the stages of development, the procedures of managing projects and the assessments analysis of the methodology are explored in this book.

PROJECT TO CHANGE MANAGEMENT

Regarding the connections of the project management procedures to change management, it is suggested that the link be from the higher level of project management work elements, such as:

- Initiate Change Management,

- Adjust Project Approach to Change,

- Control Change,

- Complete Change Management.

This is as far as most users drill into the process and generally as far as they are required to by structured analysis and designing methodologies guidelines.

DIAGRAMMATIC REPRESENTATION SHOWN

- O: Change Management Decomposition,

- O: Management of the Change Programme,

- 1: Managing of the Change Management Process,

- 2: Facilitation of the Change Management Programme,

- 3. Practising the Methodology.

O: Change Management Decomposition

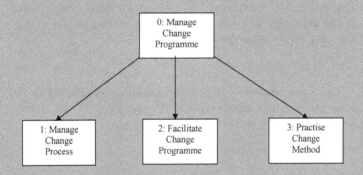

The Change Management Decomposition

The next four Dataflow Diagrams are shown on the following two pages and are:

0: Manage Change Programme,

1: Manage Change Process,

2: Facilitate Change Programme,

3: Practise Change Methodology.

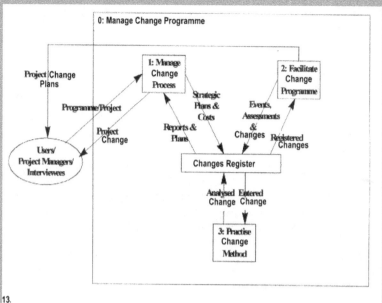

13.

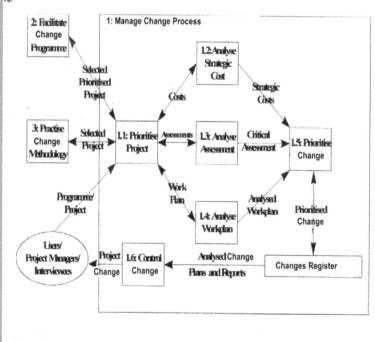

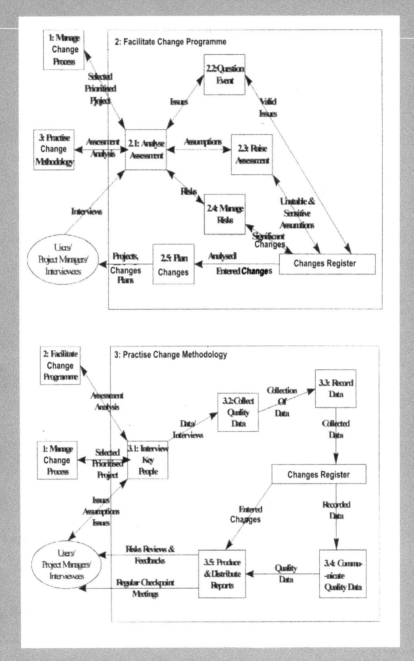

RELATIONSHIP OF DATAFLOW DIAGRAMS

All dataflow diagrams shown in above pages are based on the PsySys Limited manuals and handouts as used for the training.

DATAFLOW DIAGRAMS:	DESCRIPTION OF DIAGRAMS AND THEIR PROCESSES.
0: Manage Change Programme	• Project: something complex that you want (plan) to happen. • Change: Something that you don't want to happen. • Project management: Planning and making things happen. • Change management: Attacking anything that might disturb the plans
1: Manage Change Process	The process consists of an integrated closed loop method which logically progresses through: 1.1 Project Prioritisation, 1.2 Strategic Cost Analysis, 1.3 Assessment Analysis, 1.4 Work Plan Analysis, 1.5 Risk Prioritisation, 1.6 Change Control.
1.1 Prioritise Project	Only complex and critical projects need to have a fully structured Change Management process in place.
1.2 Analyse Strategic Cost	Strategic Cost Analysis provides a means of assessing the cost Change in a project in its very early stages and "kick-starts" the Change Management process.
1.3 Analyse Assessment	Fundamentally, projects only fail due to two reasons either the wrong assumptions were made or the significance of the assumptions was not understood.

1.4 Analyse Work plan	Work Plan Analysis may be used to focus on the risky areas of detailed, multi-level project plans when time is of the essence.
1.5 Prioritise Change	Prioritisation allows the Project Manager to divert limited resources at the most critical project change.
1.6 Control Change	Changes may be attacked at both the strategic and tactical levels. Strategic approaches look for trends and underlying causes for groups of Changes. Tactical approaches take each Change at face value.
2: Facilitate Change Programme	The Change Management Programme is essentially a framework process that allows the capture of collective knowledge and viewpoints from those involved on the project, in a form that facilitates communication of events, assessments and ensures pro-active management of changes. By dramatically improving communication, Changes are avoided, or managed proactively and project objectives are delivered on time.
2.1: Analyse Assessment	The core is Assessment Analysis. This uses structured techniques to analyse project plans and identify the most sensitive assumptions that are potentially unstable, and therefore the source of greatest change.
2.2: Question Event	Events are open questions, which are holding up plans/implementation. An Event is any open question, which has been asked at the right time to which a high quality answer cannot be provided without escalation.
2.3: Raise Assessment	Making Assessments in plans closes many Events. An Assessment is a single, simple, positive or negative statement.
2.4: Manage Changes	Unstable/sensitive assumptions create changes. Significant changes need to be managed formally. Definition: A Change is a simple statement of the form:

	"IF" Assumption proves incorrect, "THEN" Describe the impact.
2.5: Plan Changes	Change Plans impact project plans. Events, Assessments, and changes are inherent in the project plans. Population of assessment and risks registers by progressing Change Plans/Main/Project Plans.
3: Practise Change Methodology	The Role of a Change Management Practitioner includes: • Interview 'Key People' within the project, • To collect 'Quality' data, • Ensure the data collected is recorded in the Change Register, • Communicate the 'Quality' data to Project staff, • Produces accurate and timely reports for meetings: • Weekly Check Point Meetings, • Change Review Boards.
3.1: Interview Key People	Identifying the right people to interview is critical to producing a comprehensive and coherent picture of the changes facing a project. So, to decide who should be interviewed, start with the project or programme organisational structure. Depending on the scope of the change assessment it may be necessary to map the organisational hierarchy to ensure that the right people are interviewed and that the risks arising are reviewed at an appropriate level.
3.2: Collect Quality Data	This function requires to: • Interview 'Key People' within the project, • Collect 'Quality' data.
3.3: Record	Having Interviewed the 'Key People' within the

Data	project and collected the 'Quality' data: • Ensure the data collected is recorded in the Change Register.
3.4: Communicate Quality Data	The interviews of 'Key People' within the project have been completed, the 'Quality' data recorded in the Change Register and communicated to Project staff, the next function is: • Facilitate and ensure the Change Management process stays on track.
3.5: Produce Reports	After the initial round of interviews, a suitable forum must be established to discuss the changes identified. The best method is to establish a specific Change Review Meeting with a representation consisting of the Change Owners and chaired by the Programme Director or the process 'champion' in the client organisation. The main function is to: • Produce accurate and timely reports for meetings, • Weekly Check Point Meetings, • Change Review Boards.

Database Of Events, Assessments, and Changes Register Description.

Data Store: Changes Register	All events, assessments, and changes captured should be held in a Changes Register. Remember, only critical assessments will be converted into changes and held in a Change Register. Thus, by filtering the assessments and consolidating them into changes, all information captured will be rationalised and details of their source and

consequences will be traceable.

ASSETS IDENTIFICATION

The purpose for this process is for the identification of those assets of the project that need to be made into configuration items, and to control those items throughout the lifecycle. Also, to follow the Configuration Management procedures defined for the project and to ensure the version of each configuration item that applies to the development, test and live environments is known.

Configuration Management ensures that any changes applied to any configuration item are tracked and are auditable. It allows periodic baselines to be drawn where configuration items synchronise and the whole project is in a 'known state'.

The level of formality required, to be applied to configuration management must be commensurate with the size, nature and importance of the project. The approach to configuration management will be documented in the Project Plan and must be in place before major development starts, that is, at the end of Business Study.

RELEASE PROCEDURES

Configuration management has a close relationship with change control and release procedures. If a configuration management tool is used, then ensure that staff is trained in its use. Define which products from each phase are to be placed under configuration management. Involve the release management team as early as possible as they will have an interest in the Configuration Management strategy adopted for the project.

Configuration Management is particularly important throughout development when using an iterative approach. Therefore, how staff will be made aware of the configuration management tools, procedures, etc. when they join the project.

At the end of the Business Study the Prioritised Requirements List, Business Area Definition and System Architecture Definition should all be base-lined. These products will still evolve through the remainder of the project. Keep the Trace ability Matrix from the beginning. If projects are developing iteratively, consider producing a daily software build as a way of base-lining the system and identifying integration problems.

CRITICAL PROJECTS

Consult the Configuration Management Team before and during your project. Use the database under the care of the Configuration Management Team and follow the instructions in the guidelines especially concerning configuration baseline contents and the minimum baseline. Project technical documents may be stored and published.

TANGIBLE FIXED ASSETS

Tangible fixed assets should be valued at the lower of replacement cost and recoverable amount. Recoverable amount is defined as the higher of net realisable value and value in use. This can be expressed diagrammatically. The replacement cost for different classes of assets is described in the following paragraphs.

Impairment occurs where the recoverable amount falls below replacement cost. The replacement cost for operational land and buildings exists use value. In the case of specialised properties or properties not normally traded on the open market, valuation on this basis may be inappropriate and/or impractical and such property should be valued on the basis of depreciated replacement cost.

OPERATIONAL ASSETS

Other (non-property) operational assets should be valued on the basis of depreciated replacement cost. The normal basis of valuation may not be appropriate if a modern substitute is markedly different in its cost, life, or output, or where technological advances have resulted in likely replacements having significantly improved quality or quantity of outputs. Under such circumstances, it will be necessary to undertake an "equivalent asset" calculation to arrive at a replacement cost the asset.

Impairment occurs where the recoverable amount of an asset is lower than its replacement cost.

NON-PROFIT ACTIVITIES

The not-for-profit nature of the vast majority of activities means that value in use is not measurable in terms of income. In these cases, value in use will be assumed to be at least equal to the cost of replacing the service potential provided by the asset, unless there has been a reduction in that service potential.

Such a reduction can arise for various reasons, including:

• The purpose for which the asset was acquired is no longer carried;

• Out and there is no alternative use for the asset;

• The asset is to be sold;

- The asset cannot be used;
- The asset is otherwise surplus and has no alternative use;
- The asset is over-specified for its current use.

The recoverable amount will be the asset's net realisable value, i.e. the amount at which the asset could be disposed of, less any disposal costs.

Consideration should also be given to the residual value of assets created during the project, at the end of the appraisal period.

DISPOSAL OF ASSETS

Disposal of assets, especially high value assets and property, needs to be conducted with the same scrupulous rigour as the acquisition of those assets. For major assets, the process of disposal follows the stages where decisions about investment are made in the context of achieving an appropriate return for the release of the asset.

RELEASE

The purpose for this activity is to group all the individual products of the project (code, training docs, new business procedures etc) together into a coherent configured whole. The ultimate purpose for this is to perform the final test on the configured release.

Testing must be integrated throughout the lifecycle. This is not the first time the whole system has been system tested. As long the previous testing has been integrated properly this final test should be very quick and not find many additional bugs.

The final test must address all elements of the product. This will include code, installation procedures, and training documents, changed business procedures.

The process to be used for release will differ, depending on the type of application being delivered by the project. For example: Electronic Self Service programme have defined a process suitable for their applications.

RELEASE PLANS

The release plans should provide the ability to indicate where a particular requirement has been designed, built and tested. The Project Configuration Management Plan (sub-product of Project Plan) should document the approach the project will take to manage the project's assets.

As such the following activities should be included:

- Identify the roles to be involved in performing configuration management;

- Identify any tools that may be used to facilitate the management procedures;

- Describe the procedures that will be used to perform configuration and change management.

DOCUMENTATION

Project documentation that satisfies the Change Management process must be included and identified. Definitive documents must be visible to the project and Reviewers. If it is to be a model for others it must be visible programme wide and all documentation must be under version control. All changes must be documented and there must be a register of published documents.

Project Software Repository Source code should be readable by only those who need to know and such software should be subject to an audit trail of who has, who amended etc. All software should be uniquely identifiable and versioned.

The level of formality required, to be applied to configuration management must be commensurate with the size, nature and importance of the project. The approach to configuration management will be documented in the Project Plan and must be in place before major development starts, that is, at the end of Business Study. Configuration management has a close relationship with change control and release procedures. If a configuration management tool is used then ensure that staff is trained in its use.

DEFINITION OF PRODUCTS

Define which products from each phase are to be placed in configuration management. Involve the release management team as early as possible as they will have an interest in the Configuration Management strategy adopted for the project.

PROCUREMENT

'Procurement' means the whole process of acquisition from third parties (including the logistical aspects) and covers goods, services and construction projects. This process spans the whole life cycle from initial concept and definition of business needs through to the end of the useful life of an asset or end of a services contract. Both conventionally funded and more innovative types of funded projects are included. The process is not limited to the purchasing function in organisations and is inherently multi-functional especially in large, complex procurements.

REVIEWS

Any Process will define review points throughout the lifecycle of acquisition projects. Reviews are undertaken for procurement projects of all levels of change. Requests for Reviews are initiated by Senior Responsible Owners.

Additional interim Reviews may sometimes be carried out during the life of a procurement project. For a big project that has a long time span between Reviews, an additional Review may be arranged before a significant decision point e.g. the announcement of a preferred supplier). Additional reviews may also be beneficial where added assurance is needed or where there are specific areas of concern. These reviews are often referred to as Peer Reviews.

A Review is held before key decision points in the lifecycle of a procurement project. The review teams are made up of independent experienced practitioners who bring their prior knowledge and skills to bear to identify the key issues that need to be addressed for the project to succeed. The review criteria are established and published in a set of workbooks available on an intranet and website. The work of a Review team is for the project, and ownership of the review report and recommendations lies with this team.

A Review is carried out over a period of 4-5 days at the most with the review report presented and discussed with the team before the review team leaves the client premises.

AUDIT

Internal Audit primarily provides an independent and objective opinion to the Accounting Officer on change management, control and governance, by measuring and evaluating their effectiveness in achieving an organisation's agreed objectives. In most organisational bodies Internal Audit reports go directly to the Accounting Officer (Chief Executive). In order for Internal Audit to provide the Accounting Officer with an objective opinion, the Chief Executive and the Audit Committee develop an audit strategy in consultation with, and subject to approval.

The audit plan is circulated to senior members of the organisation and advance notice will be given prior to the commencement of a review. Under normal circumstances Terms of Reference will be produced for each audit assignment and these will be discussed and agreed with management. The views and opinions of management will be obtained at the end of each review and the final report will contain an agreed action plan, which will contain the name of the of the officer responsible for each recommendation and a target date for full implementation.

REVIEW PROCESS

In short, to secure the release of dual key monies, it has to be demonstrated that:

1.   The programme is aligned with the strategy,

2.   They are implementing the recommendations in the report for the projects within each programme,

3.   They have plans in place to realise the benefits of the investment.

Much of the evidence needed to meet these criteria is capable of being derived from two complementary processes:

1.   The development of business strategies,

2.   The various Reviews.

The Change Management process is designed as an aid to companies rather than as an external audit of projects.

DIFFERENCE OF PROGRAMME AND PROJECT

A project is a particular way of managing activities to deliver specific products over a specified period of time and within defined cost and resource constraints. A programme is a management framework for co-ordinating related projects and work-streams to deliver strategic outcomes and benefits over timescales that are often less well defined.

A strategic assessment is designed to apply at the start of an acquisition programme and may be repeated at subsequent key decision points. A Review can confirm that the appropriate project structure is in place and that interdependencies have been recognised.

Reviews apply to each of the procurement projects within the programme. A repeat Review later in the life of a programme can be helpful to re-visit and confirm the business case, the management of the programme changes and interactions between the projects and the delivery of benefits for the programme as a whole.

Financial value is only one of the factors to consider when deciding on the level of change faced by a programme or project. This is recognised within the Change Assessment. The fact that a programme or project environment has been deemed appropriate indicates that there is uniqueness to the programme or project, which, in turn, indicates a level of inherent change. For example, the programme or project could be of low cost but, if unsuccessful, could have a major impact upon staff morale within an organisation. Reviews are scaleable. Acquisition programmes and procurement projects should, therefore, receive a level of Review appropriate to the level of change associated.

Organisations should use Change Management and Assessment to determine the change level of their programmes and projects and to understand the nature of the changes associated with them in a structured and systematic way. Programmes or projects classified as needing small change are likely to contain significant procurements.

In certain cases, a Process was originally set up to help procurement projects that involve external (actual) expenditure. However, even on projects being "developed in house", there would normally be additional expenditure on hardware, software, licensing, increased network capacity, consultancy support. The change analysis would, of course, indicate whether to involve further reviews or whether it is small change and carried out by in house staff (and of course it is arguable that "in house developments/solutions" are smaller changes given that the client has to retain financial, technical and managerial changes compared to outsourced deals).

To summarise, technically non-procurement activities are out of the scope, but this takes a very narrow view of the benefits that can arise from a review (assurance that the project likely to be successful or, if not, remedial actions proposed).

Pilot procurement projects have the same characteristics as other procurement projects. The fact that a pilot is being managed within a project structure itself indicates that there is a unique environment, which, in turn, indicates a level of inherent risk. An assessment review should be completed in the usual way to determine the risk associated with the project.

Projects utilising existing contractual arrangements will still benefit from the added value provided by the process of reviewing and assessing, in that the majority of the issues addressed will still apply. In these cases Reviews may be scaled down where the procurement strategy is largely predetermined and standard procedures exist for the take on of new work packages.

As usual reviews start up operability and the results achieved and lessons learnt. There is evidence that anything less than a well disciplined use of framework contracts with sound management processes akin to any project leads these contracts to becoming a leaky sieve for companies and a source of high margins to suppliers. With the growth of framework arrangements it is mandatory for such call offs in central civil government and international organisations to be exposed to the appropriate level of Reviews.

A successful company would provide sufficient staff to the pool to cover the resourcing of procurement reviews. Staff will need to be trained and accredited as reviewers. You need to assign a coordinator to administer the reviews, the process roll out of changes within projects, the staff provision and the communications and training programme in house. Changes are undertaken by the Review Team Leader and nominated members.

The Project Manager should arrange an initial assessment meeting. The purpose of the assessment meeting is to agree the change level of the project (low, medium or high), to enable those responsible for the individual changes to gain an understanding of the programme/project and to establish readiness for solutions to the problems.

Notice is required following the assessment meeting in order to assemble a review team and hold the necessary prior Planning Meeting. The revised assessment may indicate a change to the change level associated with the programme or project and therefore a change to subsequent handling within the process. In that eventuality the team will discuss the way forward.

The Review Planning Meeting has, following senior staff support, been established as essential to the delivery of reviews of changes I the various projects. It is designed as a facilitated workshop at which the Senior Responsible Owner, review team and project team jointly plan their approach to the review. The planning meeting is envisaged as a mandatory part of all new reviews of changes.

The value of these planning meetings is such that only (as an example) the Programmes Director/Manager for the project/s has the authority to modify this policy. The Programmes Director/Manager may recommend earliest and continued intervention to increase the likelihood of success. The team/s involved will then agree an overall traffic light assessment for inclusion in the report at the end of each review.

TRAFFIC LIGHTS

The definitions of the 'traffic lights' are:

Red – To achieve success the programme or project should take remedial action immediately. It means 'fix the changes/key problems fast', not 'stop the project'.

Amber – The programme or project should go forward with actions on recommendations to be carried out before the next review.

Green – the programme or project is on target to succeed but may benefit from the uptake of the recommendations.

Reports and reviews should be conducted on a confidential basis. This approach promotes an open and honest exchange between the programme/project and review teams delivering maximum added value. Responsibility for the quality of the workshop and ownership of the materials used will remain with Programmes Director/Manager.

An interim review can be conducted between two major reviews, where there are interim decision points e.g. one at preferred bidder stage and the other at best and final offers. For property/construction projects, the interim reviews could be at outline design and detailed design.

MANAGING REQUIREMENTS CHANGES

This briefing looks at an issue that is fundamental to the success of any commercial relationship that is to succeed over time, the ability to accommodate change successfully. Managing the change at the end of the requirements contract is perhaps the biggest challenge of all.

Changes to requirements can be small adjustments to existing service specifications, planned modular/incremental developments, major business change leading to completely new services - or anything in between. In the context of this briefing, changes are significant enough to require management involvement.

The need to negotiate change is a continuing and ongoing component of service contracts. The ability to accommodate change successfully is fundamental to the success of any commercial arrangement that is to succeed over time; partnerships are increasingly seen as a way of coping with uncertainty, as their purpose is to accommodate change effectively and efficiently. The need to negotiate change is a continuing and on-going component of partnerships. It may be an important issue too in more conventional contractual arrangements.

PARTNERSHIP ARRANGEMENT

This briefing assumes a partnership arrangement, but the principles apply generally. Maintenance of existing systems involves ongoing changes to requirements. It is a major cost that requires careful attention.

Business managers and service providers are responsible for identifying the need for change in response to user demand or changes in the business. Service providers manage the implementation and provision of new or updated services. There may be an informed customer role providing the interface between the customer and provider. In addition, there may be programme/project teams who are involved in modular or incremental change.

REQUIREMENTS FOR CHANGE

The requirements/drivers for change during the term of the requirements contract can derive from a range of internal or external sources.

Internal change could include:

- Evolving business requirements,

- Changes in the customer's roles/responsibilities,

- Statutory developments,

- Boundary of responsibility changes,

- Rationalisation of roles,

- New developments,

- Provider restructuring, merger or acquisition,

- Revised management, reporting and/or approvals chains,

- Significant revisions to the corporate strategy/business,

- External sources of change, such as developments in technology,

- Economic trends which affect the profitability/value for money,

- The need to provide electronic forms of service delivery,

- **Meet customer expectation.**

CHANGE CONTROL PROCEDURE

A single change control procedure should apply to all changes, although there may be certain delegated or shortened procedures available in defined circumstances – such as delegated budget tolerance levels within which a manager would not have to seek senior management approval. However, flexibility needs to be built into this procedure to deal with issues such as emergencies.

A change control procedure should provide a clear set of steps and clearly allocated responsibilities covering:

- **Requesting changes,**

- **Assessment of impact,**

- **Prioritisation and authorisation,**

- **Agreement with provider,**

- **Control of implementation,**

- **Documentation of change assessments and orders.**

AUTHORISATION

Responsibility for authorising different types of change will often rest with different people, and documented internal procedures will need to reflect this. In particular, changes to the overall contract, such as changes to prices outside the scope of agreed price variation mechanisms must have senior management approval.

In many cases it will be possible to delegate limited powers to authorise minor changes, which affect particular services or Service Level Agreements using agreed processes.

Change during the term of a contract can be categorised as follows:

- **Planned/routine change,**

- **Proactive change programmes,**

- **Unplanned change.**

PLANNED CHANGE

This could include modular and incremental developments, such as planning for changes to user requirements, refurbishment of workspace, maintenance/enhancements to existing systems or planned technology refreshment. This type of change is most easily accommodated under, and is best suited to, formal change management processes.

Well-constructed contractual agreements should express provisions detailing the procedures to be adopted in initiating, discussing and delivering change through:

- User groups,

- Change control boards,

- Formal approvals processes,

- Benefits management regimes.

The procedures to be adopted for the escalation and resolution of disputes that may arise, such as:

- Defined escalation routes and timescales,

- Alternative dispute resolution procedures (neutral advisors, expert determination, arbitration),

The procedure for making amendments to the contract documentation:

- QA procedures (including legal QA),

- Authorisations (individual authorised signing powers)

- Audit trail.

PRO-ACTIVE CHANGE PROGRAMMES

Change need not necessarily always be reactive in nature. It can be initiated deliberately as a proactive approach. There could, for example, be an element of business transformation to drive forward a change programme. In this way the contract is used as a vehicle to deliver efficiency improvements and associated cost savings from the re-engineering of the customer's internal business processes, facilitated by the use of technology.

The details of approaches taken in each project to date have been different, but a typical partnership arrangement might be (in summary):

- Step 1: provider proposes business change project to customer,

- Step 2: customer approves project on basis of agreed cost/benefit model,

- Step 3: provider develops and implements new service to support new business process (at provider's risk),

- Step 4: implement and adopt new business processes,

- Step 5: both parties measure resultant cost savings to customer using agreed cost/benefit model,

- Step 6: provider's service charges calculated as a percentage of realised cost savings to customer.

Recent contracts show an emerging trend. Over the life of partnership as a whole, the expectation of the parties, sometimes underwritten by contractual guarantees from the provider, is that the aggregate cost savings to the customer over the term of the partnership may in fact exceed the aggregate 'core' service payable by the customer. The viability/appropriateness of approach outlined above of course depends on the nature of the partnership, the customer organisation (in terms of its receptiveness to change, potential for improvement in existing business processes etc), and the services to be delivered.

UNPLANNED CHANGE

Unplanned change is imposed on the partnership from outside (for example, resulting from a change in some aspect of the external environment). This is the most difficult type of change to manage and accommodate. It is also potentially the most damaging to the partnership. It can hit the partnership unannounced and require immediate action by both parties. At worst it can serve to invalidate the deal for one or both parties, resulting in unplanned conclusion of the programme or even the partnership.

Unplanned change will test the strength of the partnership relationship, and the capabilities of its management. The response to un-planned change is crucial and must be structured. In response to unplanned change, the partnership (that is both parties in co-operation), must undertake the following analysis:

- Step 1: understand and assess the impact of the change on partnership. Can this be dealt with under the existing change management procedures or does this require specialised management?

- Step 2: escalate within both partner organisations as appropriate,

- Step 3: review the basis of the deal – does the original deal remain viable for both parties?

- Step 4: assess the extent of change required to the deal,

- Step 5: negotiate the required amendments.

From the customer's perspective as the public sector partner a key decision point is often reached at Step 4 above. It may be necessary for both partners to make real, and sometimes significant, concessions in the resulting negotiations in order to make the deal work for the future. A complete audit trail of developments is essential to ensure public accountability, but you must be prepared to make bold judgments where necessary to ensure the survival of the partnership (subject to the overall deal remaining viable to the public sector partner). Your decision-making must be driven by clear business objectives of the organisation.

MAIN CHANGE MANAGEMENT POINTS

A change is an uncertain event, which may have an adverse effect on the project's objectives. Using Change Management should be very effective in the quest for identifying changes throughout the project lifecycle.

Remember, Change Management is:

•   Forward looking, investigating problems and how to deal with threats,

•   A tool enabling communication, getting people at all levels to talk to each other and to interact,

•   A no blame team culture, bringing concerns into the open where actions can be taken and plans put in place, in order to stop a change occurring.

IDENTIFICATION OF RISKY PROJECTS

The Change Management process commences by identifying the enterprises most important and risky projects, as these must be given priority. Change Management is essentially a method that permits the collection of knowledge and experience from those involved, in a form that facilitates the Systematic Interaction and Generic Methodology for Applications:

SYSTEMATIC

The varied events, their assessments, and the consequential risks relating to or consisting of a system. Methodical in procedures and plans, these are addressed to those involved and deliberating within the parameters of their systems development responsibilities. The results will depend on interaction.

INTERACTION

The mutual or reciprocal action which encourages those involved in the programmes and projects to communicate with each other and to work closely with a view to solving the threatening events before they impact on the development of the system. The individuals involved maintain a generic approach.

GENERIC APPROACH

Relates and characterises the whole group of those involved in assessing the events and attacking the threatening ones, before they become risks to the development of the system. The end result being the avoidance of apparent problems, within the pre-defined users systems requirements. This is enabled by following the establish methodology.

METHODOLOGY

The system architects and the change management practitioners simply follow the approved body of systems development methods, rules and management procedures employed by their organisation. For practical or even ethical reasons, it must be noted that with such a philosophy, it is seldom possible to fulfil all requirements of very large organisational systems. As such, the Change Management methodology ought to be obligatory and as such it should be administered in all applications.

APPLICATIONS

Putting to use such techniques and in applying the change management principles in the development of various applications will involve numerous and varied activities. A concrete issue in developing new applications is the problem of communication among the people involved, the motivation constantly needed for generic work, the ability to interact systematically and in using a structured systems methodology.

CONFIGURATION, RELEASE, ASSETS

Change Management and the changes to Configuration, Release, and Assets as a whole group of activities have traditionally been concerned with finding effective solutions to specific operational problems. The purpose of this book is to look at current problems and new, better methods, techniques, and tools for processing changes. In the past, it has been found that too many of the solutions are not implemented and, of those that are, too few survive the inclination of client functional areas to return to familiar ways of doing things. Therefore, Change Management personnel have gradually come to realise that their tasks should not only include solving specific problems but also designing problem-solving and implementation systems that predict and prevent future problems, identify and solve current ones, and implement and maintain these solutions under changing conditions.

COMPONENTS OF CHANGES

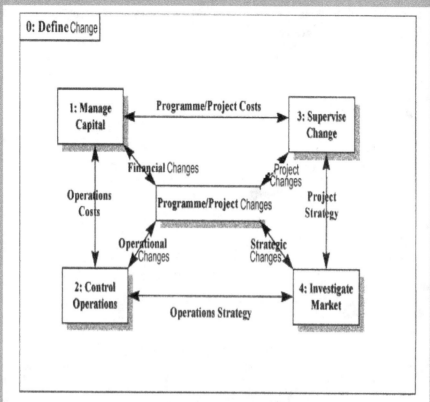

The Comp[onents Of The Total Business Changes

BIBLIOGRAPHY:

A Sofroniou, The Management Of Commercial Computing, PsySys Limited, ISBN: 0 9527956 0 4.

A Sofroniou, Structured Management Techniques, Association For Psychological Counselling And Training, Training Material, 1984.

A Sofroniou, Structured Systems Methodologies, Published and unpublished lecture notes, 1987 -1997.

A Sofroniou, Management Styles lectures, 1982.

A Sofroniou, Thesis submission on Automotive Components and Materials Purchasing System for Engineering Qualifications, 1983.

A Sofroniou, Collaborative project on Knowledge-base, Expert Systems and Artificial Intelligence, with Imperial College, Logica plc and The Engineering Industry Training Board, 1985-1986.

A Sofroniou, Rapid Structured Methodology for Life Assurance Systems, 1990-1992.

A Sofroniou, Analysis and Design project on EPoS Retail and Logistic System, 1995.

A Sofroniou, Research project, a study on COTS (Commercial Off The Shelf) Packages, 1995.

A Sofroniou, Technical Design projects for Internet Integration, Security, Client/Servers, Data Warehousing and Databases, 1996-1997.

A Sofroniou, The Year 2000 Project and Planning Procedures for European Group of Companies, 1998.

Ian Graham, Object Oriented Methods, Addison Wesley, ISBN: 0 201 56521 8.

E Yourdon and L Constantine, Structured Design, Yourdon inc., 1975.

Chris Gane and Trish Sarson, Structured Systems Analysis: Tools and Techniques, Improved System Technologies, Inc., 1977.

www.ingramcontent.com/pod-product-compliance
Lightning Source LLC
Chambersburg PA
CBHW061033050326

40689CB00012B/2796